GROUND LEVEL

ALSO BY JENNIFER RAHIM

Poetry
Mothers Are Not the Only Linguists
Between the Fence and the Forest
Approaching Sabbaths
Redemption Rain

Fiction
Songster and other Stories

JENNIFER RAHIM

GROUND LEVEL: POEMS

PEEPAL TREE

First published in Great Britain in 2014
Peepal Tree Press Ltd
17 King's Avenue
Leeds LS6 1QS
UK

ISBN 13: 9781845232054

Supported by
ARTS COUNCIL
ENGLAND

CONTENTS

Dream

An island rests in me, almost reachable, as dreams journey to destinations mapped in sleep – no cloud. That is their promise – the visions dreams parent. To dream, if you believe, is to deliver a god. In this womb of flowering rock we have birthed many. And maybe that multitude is as it should be. Gods are what we dream – to hold faith with the real.

Seismic

There is no timing this moment of shake
down. Even christopher knew it when his maps
failed the fissure of lost \
broke his world. The ripped veil
of every temple we make will surely come.
Will too redeem the ground
we plant sword and cross upon.
Every God dies to rise from this.
So it will come the first
imperceptible rumble way down
while fat sizzles and rum warms.
Whatever its form: leakage of Ibis red
a single shoe
thrown in Cairo 1 degree rise
on the barometer a fist to heaven
a cry that shatters a glass sky
a NO like Rosa's and Malala's.
There is no real timing it. Syria
awaits it. Port-of-Spain too
will meet it standing by a lighthouse
begging for even silver. The word
that trips makes giants fall
reach a rope-end-day
from the mouth of babes. It will split
any rock. Like the one coin
of that woman emptied to nothing
every treasure guarded. It will
make a gulf of no return. Too late.
Paradise missed.
Haiti 2010 was a sign not for *them* –
for us who stand
on solid ground waiting
for shaded ships to come in
shipping out unholy cargoes

promising pleasure like bleached beaches
that sell islands out
trade in wind-
falls gateway for continents
to pass on whatever the colour of yellow.
But they will come the stirrings
from the deep that return
the drowned devi
roll away the stone
of the crucified one.
Fault lines will break every sentence
In their time will
ask the question: on what ground.
Yes, a single line of verse
a Word
can ROCK
a universe.

On Quitting Columbus

just when I decide to quit
Columbus

write his name off my list
of complaints

shake the dust from my feet
like the saved

that story end-up like a cliché
on my page

only this time the players
switch sides

ups and declare the state a jail
for a salvation mission

to hook criminals while Crime
living free

behind gated communities
tight security,

watching the movie, safe
from *them*

that drag-out, handcuff
parade of black

with back broad enough
to carry fault for everybody

make it hard to let History sail,
bury the hatchet

when the track look the same –
a rerun from another age

or a language playing dead only
to ambush change

Six-dollar High

red band maxi
en route to the city,

keeping time
to the road's zesty line.

the driver, a real cutie
born-again-wanna-be

Usher, watching we
watch he lock down

and shades up,
loving his cool air-

condition ride
from Arima,

lavender fresh
piping through the vents,

we sailing easy
in three o'clock

beat
        down
heat

TIME BANDIT
eating the Priority.

inside is grey-
tint-comfort, clean

semi-recline seats,
alleluia non-stop on CD

and before eye
could blink twice we fly

by Curepe's madman
pantomime,   past

the brewery where Carib
brand is sky,

then the woman
stranded by the *Quazay*

begging for a ride –
addict dry –

but the twenty-four seater
close its eyes, praying

for the green, praying:
race on BANDIT,

don't stand here, brother
juice the accelerator,

don't stop this smooth
six-dollar high.

A Fish Tale

Miss, yuh shoulda be there
to see dem Big Fish dance
like they have no worries.
Friday and we dodging de guard
'cause to tell the honest truth
Sheriff boat not authorize
and SoE harassing everybody.
Is honest living we making, Miss,
and life hard – even fish
in lockdown.
Doh get mih wrong.
I not blind
and PO-lice too
have to eat ah food.
But Miss, ocean have plenty road
so we stay clear ah the avenue
dem bandit travel on.
I see it with mih two eye.
Moon full and dem Big Fish
happy as pappy, playing
theyself, drinking
Johnny Blue, smoking
Cuba and walking on water.
That is what I see.
Sheriff and Illegal with me
but they doh believe.
Nothing biting and time boring
so they relax
and sleep fall, braps!
Not me. Sea is no bed
for human being.
And, Miss,
dem Big Fish dance!
Smiling currency.

Things nice. The Law
only catching small-fry.
And, I not bragging,
but I too have a t'eory
though I never go UWee.
I giving you one likkle hint:
how Jesus walk on water
have nothing to do with how
dem Big Fish gallery
like they hit ah Vincy.
Trus' me.

Write . Light

In this place poets hurt
enough to die
though God is a nationality,
a name *discovery* ordained
a doctrine of Three.

But this is a place where
the WORD
is born
to no real company,
even at the microphone
poetry is a flugtag affair
that wins laughs while we drown
gasping gagged air –

innocence muzzled
while we bribe time
to praise the lie

while we chase seconds
to destinations with no arrivals,
numbed to felled lives, limbs
bleeding on the roadside,

while we   free-
dive
on a Red Bull high,   BLIND
to the litter
behind the altar
at Columbus Square.

No one hears
the measure of shadow
in any rhythm:

Victor's down
BEAT
          or
Roach's blunt question
to witness:
          a requiem in readiness.

Who dares count
the   DUM
syllables bearing down
a craft's discipline to hope?

In this country
I know the beat
by which poets die.

I write and
write to meet
the light.

Dear Editor

To: religiousnews@tstt.tt
Subject: request
Attachment: Pelicans at Evening

Dear Editor
For your kind consideration.

PS
1. I am the author of the attached poem but you may follow your usual protocol and not respond.
2. This is a poem born from a promise that, I predict, even the Magi will have time to visit; but you are free to follow your usual protocol and not respond.
3. This is a poem that chose me to help carry its cross so that you may follow your usual protocol and not respond.
4. This is a poem that wept over its city and moved on – but you may follow your…
5. This is a poem whose face I wiped with a page but you could follow your usual protocol and…
6. This is a poem that mourns a light to your salvation so please go right ahead and follow your own…
7. This poem is in the tomb of your refusal to roll back its great stone and discover it is already risen, but you are free – to not respond…

Friendly Exchange

caribpress@uk.com
triniwriter@gmail.com

Curfew, September, 2011

Hello Writer

I hope all is well with you and the new book develops apace. I write to ask you to consider participating in a project designed to resurrect a deceased poet from your region. He is not Trini so you may not be familiar with his work. I however predict the mission will interest you. Find flyer attached. It outlines what I am trying to do.

Best wishes
Publisher

triniwriter@gmail.com

Dear Publisher

Thank you for your e-mail. The book has taken a different turn since the SoE. The crisis is much larger than it seems. I am very busy shaping the season's hurt so I will have to decline your invitation, as worthy as your project sounds. I might add that it may surprise you to know I am somewhat familiar with the writer you propose to remember – although our nationalities do differ. Where my curiosity lies is with your prediction about my interest in your venture.

Best
Writer at Work

caribpress@uk.com
Dear Writer

Thank you for sharing the progress of your work. I look forward to the outcome. I regret you cannot participate in my project and about that link: I think you share with the poet in question a meritorious risk-taking in writing. As to the SoE, as far as I am aware, there has not been a single report in the UK press or broadcast media – which rather shows where the Caribbean lies in British affections. One would like to say astonishing, but the silence is sadly unsurprising.

Do take care
Publisher

triniwriter@gmail.com

Dear Publisher

Yes, it is unsurprising that British media (inter alia) would be uninterested in an SoE in one of its old colonies, as it would be surprising if I were not well-briefed on the recent burning of London, which is to say: I am even more familiar with black British dissent than with a writer from a former Caribbean colony who also happens not to be Trini. But what one might say is also not astonishing is that I am genuinely grateful that your press does not share British disaffection for the Caribbean. The real no brainer is that the Ungod of things has not much changed – now that is a prediction, had you made it, would have been right on the egg.

Cheers
Writer at Work

PS: No doubt critics will judge this to be *not a poem* but I am trying to live up to the "risk taking" bit which, as you say, forced the connection between myself and the poet in question. I trust you will appreciate my upgrade from the letter form to an e-mail exchange and that I chose to stay clear of evoking any “classic” ghosts (though both Heathcliff and Catherine would have been tricky tropes). Anyway, all this makes me at least not dead and grateful for your correction of my typos.

PS (again): I hope you remain interested in *my* project– but that, I cannot predict!

Lines to Fanon I

You insisted you spoke for your time.
Well, it is now, Fanon. Like foolish masons,
we build on the sand of false hierarchies,
prejudices of all kinds mixed with mortar,
walls erected to divide, not house us all –
strangers to each other.
Listen, the earth is noisy with the hell
of its construction: nations clone democracy
with war, religions sacrifice faith to dogma,
innocence murdered on the altar
of horrid passions.
Carrion time, brother!
No people here, just a sad company of ghosts
huddled together, doors bolted, keeping dry
from the storm of our colossal failure
to love larger than any creed
we venerate or hate.
                                        Pray, imperfect saint,
we finally leap the gate.

Lines to Fanon II

The world is not as you desired, brother.
Maybe you never expected its arrival,
but worked hope into a language large
as metaphor – the one faith that transports
vision across hardened lines that gird us
in plots much too small for the universe
coursing, seamless, through your blood.
The world is not as you imagined it.
You were too soon, and we too late.
So we are a drag-foot humanity, destined
to lament the kingdom almost possible.
No, we are not the stars you dreamed
to touch, pure radiances unfettered
by any past – barring vision –
like bright-eyed children, at last.

Turn from Dark

Who will guard
the season's turn
from dark when we sell
so cheaply the sky's silver?

Who will make noise,
point the accusing finger,
risk losing a head
for those fallen among us?

Who will dare stir Carter?
Write, now, the poetry of bread,
put aside decency's level
to stand in rank with poems
that bawl-out, shout
what even the trees will un-bare
in the ravaged belly of Matura?

Those poems will come   spit fire
like that father –
crowned with his dread
authority
let his word
                                drop
on the conscience of a nation,
demanding justice
for more
than his *no-saint* son:

"Not so! Not PO-lice,
        NO-BODY

must take
a life so"

his right grief rattling
every undefended bone
while we watch the screen

DUMB

My First Last Poem

This is definitely my first
last poem.

Here it is. Read. Look

under its dress. Feel
its breasts.

Now name it.
Better still, make it *your*

discovery – hold
it down.

Dazzle yourself
as lines catch your light.

Then plant a claim
in its flesh. Evangelize it.

Baptize the bastard
in whatever name

you know that makes you
best. Write – object-

ively – its history. Now
read it that story.

Teach it *your* ABC:
intonation,

declension, rules of
conjugation.

Satisfied? Yes.

So now, look –
like a God it slips

from your grasp.
What now?

Betray, deny, crucify,
pierce its side,

add a great stone
to keep it down.

Guess what?
It goes on.

Fitting the Bill

Here's that poem you have been waiting on, / making an entrance wearing preferably chiffon/ jazzy blue/ and flaring fishtails / so the whole get-up /glides in, gleaming stars / and water at once; / and this is the one / with her heart in her hands, / mascara on the brink / of a run, so she steps perilously / on white stilettoes/ that glitter rhinestone / announcing her, a tick /
tocking sensation circumscribed / by past (perfect) tenses / as she advances with him / under her skin / leaving in her wake / a storm of fragrances / windblown / glossy pages / that sell her out, / at least, not cheaply; / but her fingers, thankfully, / are already her mother's, /dusted with pollen and smelling of onions. / No worries – / they confirm her/ strong.

Ground Doves in the Lime Tree

("No sound is dissonant which tells of Life"
Samuel Taylor Coleridge, "This Lime-Tree Bower My Prison")

He's at it again,
staunchly pruning the lime tree,
only there's no art in it.

I can barely watch –
him on top the ladder,
his head in cloud

as he snaps after branches,
even those grown
miraculously,
to correct the ruin
of the first trimming.

I could only hope
the family of ground doves
had long ago flown.

I had seen fledglings,
maybe two, nestled amid branches
barbed like their history's first
delivery to Haiti,
their fruit enlisted to bolster
the plough of Limeys
through island waters –.

The shadow of that passage
is, yet, a painful gladness.

But they are wholly native now
as those small doves dreaming

of their winged release
with a wary mother on watch.

And, that morning,
I was happy to be alone in sunlight
filtered through hardy green,
and marvelling at the miracle
our lime tree housed,
and how it had flourished
through sun and rain,
until the severed limb at base
and the clay brick
and rusty rod chucked there
to buttress the damage
were no more visible.

In that light, all the pain
there ever was to bear
seemed no cross to carry –
with the whole tree cooing
and white blossoms offering
the soon-come relief of limes.

But there he is again –
his silvers electric
in the midday glare –

working, dutifully,
at his cutting, meaning well,
but with no hands for that care,

and the tree, without song,
paring down
and a widening sky
falling where there was shade –

now

                    the startled light
                    of stripped forests.

I could not look
even after his shears shut
and he returned to ground.

But when cool evening came,
in that botched lean-to bower
with the wind-pressed profile
of an Atlantic coastline,
I heard the shuffle of feathers
and a dove calling
where few limes hung,
daring me believe
        in time's mercy.

To the executioner within

Dear Herod: I live yet you prefer me dead. What is my offence? Or better, what do you dread? Today, I refuse your grave. I sleep now to dream myself a God. When I awake, think of me as your breath.

Pelicans at Evening: I
(for Pat Bishop)

Pelicans,
as many as seven,
steadfast as pointers
press heaven,
push eastward across Toco's
unquiet run of coast.

News comes here
unhurried
as the beat
of ample wings,
holds the eye true
to evening's fall.

Now,

when an ocean's peace
is gathered into beaks
that could deliver
the miracle of a child,

I hear you are gone.

And what is this word
bequeathed us
as you pass into earth –

our souls full yet
with every
bold
and fragile
note
you shepherded to birth,

not one
orphaned
or unformed sound
left unhoused?

So Miss B.,
what is this nothing
as you go your way
to Mucurapo?

What parting gift –
your baton's final command?
Our tongues stilled,
grief left broke,
for your wanting
no more
than servant's pay,
wanting too
a sunflower's witness
at the close
of your giving days.

In this crude season
of curfew
from ourselves,
your cowbell's
chosen metre
is perfect song, you
knowing well
silence earned strikes
the purest note,
speaks clearest,
being free
of disregard,
being free, blesses
with its own question.

So, Sister Pat,
is it that you saved
your best wine
for last?

Redeemed us
from our noise?

Your passing's ripe Art –

this holy hush
as that arcane flock journeys
routinely
            home.

An Independence Echo

How to reach – each; is there such a shore, an assurance, such a reach?
We Reach is a place on a coast, an arrival we know, where
land and sea and mountain and plain, wide
open, plain, – a Paradise II, next to El Dorado… a cloud,
that pain in the… pen plainly; is arrival ever
that simple, such a shore, sure simplicity, where we,
we reach, there or here is, a plan and an anthem, dem
an' we, is a flag, doh lag, we moving…
is a doh drag… home is, is home, a home… finally? We.
Or is… is it a wave, a waving out of
reach, far from, near to, reach FOR the ST…
ARS over… never… reverse back and begin?
Is a start… have heart, but just there, is a vanish…
vanishing… point we know, tiefing dream… the promise
missed… long time we eh… is not a fête in here… Maurice and
Rodney, missed?… Should we miss…know what to miss…prefer the night,
nightmare, now and forever, ever getting there, world with, without end,
a horizon, reeling? No, not we! The promise
we shudda reach there SHUD-
dering there, orisons, for bright, brighter, for suns
set too soon for Keyana… names too many
for the few that never reach, at last,
sunny, ground, holi… like a jolly
roger… over and out, holi -day like a holiday, O Happy Day,
is a ground, a beach, each preach a
wrong… really, we? Oh not again… when is a gain History,
again… but wah wrong…? You can't see, hear, feel,
the rhythm, riddim is everything… take a lime
we is We and this place, O Lovely, is a high-
yes… down in the belly… the Rudder… is ah steering we… a thanks,
thanksgiving… is we, praise be in the wounding, is a song,
is a beat – at last… steel from rock and we, here, doh hear,
only mock and skin-teeth… sans, the flowering is, sans
humanite… is pain a pass? – Yes, King David,

we believe… our Fa-Da… who DA DEE DA… tell we
what is the measure of heaven… come back and teach we
the PRAISE. Look, we for a city, yes for a future,
wings over plains, a beauty, dim, diminish-
ing flocks reach back,
how to keep, back, the mangroves' survival, vital… So sing Molly; sing
Kubs… sing…we reach, in Truth, real, in trut' we here and root,
rooted, a route is a coming, a highway comin down,
going done de road… the load of home, home
is… is a wonder… WON, yes Independence a shake,
then a MASH UP (doh say so) the place is a striving… doh mine
the quake, 2010 an earth-quake… since 1804 the MORE… WE-in-truth…
is we lose we lamp for the way. We leave
and gone away from you. We and one…
wonderful land, yes, YES, is an island ever one, one arch, archi-
pelago, yes, ES is a verb, *is* real, a reality; we
leave that too, leave before we know that love; Cuba,
is a love, a love we never know, fail to go the full, under-full-high-
way to pass… for we 20/20 vision, was there a message to learn…?
But look we nah… hectors and hectors of green we sell out
for ah hell ah SMELTER that never pass, is ah mas', look,
ah look, de devil playing de… ah steal we, and what,
what about steel, who stealing we – children… tru-tru,
on de Hill, in Diego, de Valley, Caroni, South? Is a gun, steel, stealing
we home within reach, each,
teach we how to reach, too far from… speech.
Oh how to make a start, ah Art, in RED
futures, city of mirrors, parties of clones backing
up a shore, sure, ensure currency tief,
but *yes, yes we can*, O ma-ma, AMA,
after de *1-love* drone… is a turn, is a return…
and look, Mandela
gone… O Maria is a prayer… for all ah we
in flesh, in red, everybody eating lead,
red is a joker, Ha-Ha-La-La-Ley…
la-la… land, so we red, is a jab,

a jab-jab in yuh head, in the dance, a prance in come
and away, from me, no pain, in vibes, done, undone this, disc we
is we, and I, done with being, becoming, 50 past a 200 years beginning,
we reach, we reach, here, where – How? This shore, sure, SAL-
ve, salve? A salvation… HOW to, H-OW to reach,
each, HOW-ow-ow to reach
a nation? - OW
YELL-

Low-

ow-ow

NO

ssshoo

YELL

Oooo

how-how-OW

yell-O

O-

Shu……

Yellow or Pelicans at Evening: II

there it comes
on the brink of injured hope
with the pelican flown
comes a heart unfurled
an uplift in lengthening shadow
a light switched on
in rooms empty of reason
an upended bowl
outpouring
an umbrella in rain
canopy of sun
a benediction
in eye-water season

there it comes
a colour christening
the city's red page
a level for irradiant highs
it arrives, a note
pitched above a street's downbeat –
beauty of shell
dot of joy
erupting in all that bring-down
healing amber of undead stone
inverted bulb of tear

there it comes
to a household in lockdown
long time locked-
in fête singing
No, No we eh going home
to the guns of UN/
just response
jamming down wombs

bandits of dreams
one army too many
rivers of oh-oooo-
missions
nightmare reruns
but here it is
YELLOW
door to opening sound
saving cross of roads
motion of turn
arc of line
to promise of circle
and full pot
libation of sweetness
balm for any shape of hurt
charmer of steel
music-Lady
House of star
and bright sky-
dancer
play NOW
the Sanctus
slow

Haiti, again

Let us renounce, today, all clichés. Declare a fast. Wear ashes. No more interred words, unholy charities, keyboard theories, scapegoat theologies we brew to speak about you – never with you as though we fear your light. Even in your absence, you strip our platitudes; our transgressions scribbled in the dust of your streets; our resolve like reeds. Let there be no more post-fête-post-mortems – the indecency of sunbaked ruminations trading in catastrophe. Make this our one petition: Ayiti, steel us to come to you.

Violence

I've been noticing of late
how well we kill what we hate,
crafting fates even hell
cannot bring itself to imagine.
I've been seeing how well
we wreak terror on tyrants
then pin ourselves heroes
for rebalancing the scales –
but with what weights?
How lightly we move on lies
to the promise of better days.
                    Well, maybe *you*
can understand why, of late,
I've been looking at my hands
and feeling so afraid.

About Typos

They keep us humble –
if we can resist making
scapegoats of them.
At best, they love us enough
to burst our bubbles
and plant our feet firmly
where they belong –
on the ground.
The story runs long,
only in the beginning
they weren't called typos
but apples – slip-ups
that never let us forget
it is always, in a sense,
about language.
Who knows? An omission
(in text) may have caused
the first ever fall;
but look at the upside
of that happy mishap –
(who would have thought)
a God!
And that's why 'A' forever
sounds the fruit tagged
with pride's downfall,
if by perfection we mean
having no fault,
un-needing of any God,
or – thinking postcolonial
for the theoreticians –
being like God – the proof
(back then) possession
of the language
that pronounced 'A' an apple.

Whatever the premise,
or actual height of the fall,
apples and typos
are the same – though some
may find that leap too great.
They name us
human, and on occasion
do create A-class miracles
like the message of consolation
from a friend (after producing one
on the world wide web)
as only friends can write,
at end, *Live* for *Love*,
and be absolutely right.

feet are the level that makes the ground a chapel – altar where the eye reads all that is given, all received and lost. Or else it is the heart's rampart to regions beyond vision's horizon – seat of hope that marks the swift's passage and every vanishing point yields a star. Or else it is the gateway to the underworld roots traverse to green the universe, no flat-earther's prison in need of a discovery myth to correct. It is the level from which true travellers and seekers depart to confirm us citizens of multitudinous spheres.

It happened

It happened on feast of the sky-god. The sacred came to ground. Somehow she had missed it, maybe from straining too long at altars across an eternity of separation. But how could she, following so faithfully the seasons of crèche, communion and crucifixion? She did anyway – miss the spirit of it. But that day, the homeliness of earth welcomed her – wanted the human touch of her. It has never left – that burnished surface, pressed to wafer smoothness and polished to lamp glow. Since then, she has been busy revising her catechism. Since then, her people mistakenly weep at her grave; but if they look they would see her dancing in step with hurricanes and divining the penmanship of lightning.

Before You

Before you my world was a spectre of crosses,
an alphabet of spirit narrowed to a single sign,
the needle's-eye faith of chasubles and mitres.
God spoke in whispers before you and women
prayed for sons to usher you from heaven.
I truly believed hell was disbelief, before you.

Now, and after you, I believe my salvation
is this landscape of ever-opening doorways –
the scripture I was never taught to pray –
the sacred verses of your drums, your dance
a fierce homily warning retribution, your sound
an anointing that names me, speaking
to the very root of my faith – even before you.

Miss Miles I (in memory of Gene Miles)

So now Miss Miles, it's tiger stripes. Armour
not tough enough to fight the beast that beat
you down on city streets you walked, wired.
No fear could stitch your lips or force retreat
to ease and honeyed treats. A warner's bell
took possession of your tongue, was knife
slipped between joint and marrow, was shell-
blow, buss mark, speak out – well done that life.
Our eyes shut tight like sleep we feign so night
may pass and we awake to analgesic prayer
at altars cold of sacrifice. Your right
bleats in us like those bills we shrug and tear.
Strewn strips, the crude wreckage of a heart
we watched fall from heights you heeled to chart.

Miss Miles II

Well A-A! Is Jean we take and make prison
for what is black or white? So we stay. Doh see,
doh hear, the click-clock… trigger of a nation,
for miles. Yes, she walk *a mile and a half in she…*
across this cuffed archipelago. Even if we play
Hall's mas', a protest, a washed shame, would it
be more than *mincing fantasies…*? If we say
the *mea culpa* in ashes would it mean shit
to those we trample on? Or lock-jointed on
pacts and pay-outs, do we steal to trade truth
cheaply, and crucify every foreday spirit born
to a mas of night with no form fit to youth
again the dreams we dream to wake up sleep?

Miss Miles III

A kind kind of light lingers where roads meet
and vast rivers kiss eternal seas. If she speaks,
would she say, "There is a place for all our pain
in the mansions of sweet J'ouvert streets. So peace,
peace." In rooms decked without rhyme or
reason, a ballad cured in slow chip and ding-go-lay,
jump-up and wine-down plays on;
for every hurricane we skin-teeth and suck salt
to cross over so new meters get baptised,
and wounds, keys that open heaven. If she
could play ah mas this blue morning, amass
with us the beauty she mirrored, to stave
a dark no hat could shelter, would we carry,
like first fruits in high day, her level offering?

Miss Miles IV

In the garden, this morning,
in spring-water air
of a still new year,
I gathered limes –
the West Indian kind –
beneath branches
that found,
how I cannot tell,
the balance of bounty.

Amen. Yes, amen…

Yellow suns like yolks
in my hands
speak now of ripe mercy –
like the soon come alleluia-
avenues in costume
we wait on;
hosannas after eclipses
many-numbered as those polka dots
that riddled the morning sky
of your witnessing dress,

Miss Miles.

No matter. No bother.
I cradle limes like eggs
into a well-grilled house,
thinking of tea to break gas
as sirens bawl
through streets
cooked with song,
thinking, too, look how Papa Mas
fashioned you, for us,
oh so very large…

Emmaus
(for Keith Smith)

Keith, if words make a country
where people meet,
then it was large presence
you gave us – and is only love
could bring a word
to make a heart burn.
No lightweight saviour
could walk this Emmaus Road
or whatever name they call
this dry season of soul
when every heaven we dream
in drought. But Keith,
you leave people free to praise
the God they know
because you believe we all
in the same boat,
and is here, on this rock,
we coming out stars,
each a brightness that romance
and cutdown same time,
then turn 'round to meet us,
bag in hand, like bandit tief we hope.
That was you for we, Keith –
a man with syntax soak
in the sea's vinegar and words
that could bend corner,
breaking order like steel notes
hold ground, refusing
to make death a home.
Sentence like moko-jumbie stride
and engine-room drive
come down every Calvary
we live on – stories you too live

and bless and give to eat –
the pain and glory that is we –
tasting at times (I hear) to excess
(as if starved of your own leaven).
What I know is you make
every life a shrine,
the loud company you keep
with the questions we carry,
the missed epiphanies
that bring you to kneel,
and boy, your oiled subtleties –
the discipline of a neighbourliness
that is the gift history give,
asking that we must first be flesh,
the baptism poets search for –
a style past prejudice
like the wine of your prose,
a music sweet, as Papa Mas say,
like picoplat's song
could surprise the dawn.

Respite (for Anya)

To a stage that rivals any brand of farce, a light –
a young woman comes, a rainbow. No sign
taken for wonders hitched to dead pasts,
but witness to prophecy's advent – Walcott's
new Athens. Her field, a runway stylin'
raiment as phenomenal as the language
islands stitched from worlds made seamless
as the weave of sea her hands command
into artefact. The eye astonished as at the dawning
of a star – the bright that explodes the possible,
even as we punish time for our failure to draw
nearer the distance for which Carter's every-
child dreams: to live the *will* to change tense –
make miracle present, be blessing cup
that redeems the fault we all fit, and silences
any bench of bats eager to tie millstones
about the necks of sunbeams. Anya,
architect of how we may wear our tomorrows,
delight in this sad carnival of waste and mamaguy,
may your challenge be always what Thursdays
have come to mean for us: our colours uplifted
and the inexhaustible grace that is your name.

For Anthony McNeill on All Saints

To tell you the truth,
I've been thinking about Tony –
if he would permit that familiarity.
I met only his verse.
I've been thinking poetry
should always be brave,
or else it cannot speak, and his was,
the way true courage is –
an amity with what we fear.
Not crude disclosure,
the bogus bravado that sells
those too weak to suffer well.
No, courage is never that cheap.
It both upbraids and heals us,
makes the faithless see ghosts
in the face of what is real,
yet waits like love while we lament
what we hope dead, only so we
may never have to be brave –
if that means an apprenticeship
to the sufferer's beat.
I've been thinking of you, Tony,
and the self your lines vested
in a shining that strikes blind
our well-managed lives,
sends us stumbling in-
sight – that was your calling
to redeem us with. Tony,
I have been looking, this day,
for your light among the saints.

A Simple Apocalypse

New will be the blessing
for those who stand ahead
of their shadows,

like pointers reshuffle
the universe, divining paths
to fresh beginnings,

for in the end, all are salted
with what flesh will betray
and with what flesh

alone is ordained to bless,
so we grow to slow fullness. Here,
like there, a God must descend

our fragile rainbows
to remarry the earth, awaken
our dead, enliven our sleep

with dream. O poets
of dream say a-new-world-coming,
today. Not without yesterdays,

not without meridians
crossed to unheard sound-
altering rhythms, making life

with language – no grammar
is stone for the Word-alive –
like that line of Scripture

on the windscreen of a car
I saw plying the Paria Road:
"Who Jah Bless: No Man Curse."

It was a quality of faith
the owner flaunted, not the car,
but his high favour.

Newness will arrive,
a simple apocalypse,
ordinary bread,

like the woman whose name
I remember less
than the unchurched wisdom

she left for my journey on
that Sunday morning,
when I saw her great age

bent like a comma
on the road's side, standing
there, resigned to hope –

the prayer that made me stop,
and as she laboured in
like heavy time, said,

"This body not strong again,
but I put myself in place
ready for the up-take."

The miracle of her word!
Its minted radiance echoing
another arrival, as real

as her ritual going to Cumana
where her altar waited –
a station to her heaven.

I was only her *transport*
but taken-up by the beauty
she became. So the *light*

of the world lives on,
and when she alighted
for her Mass said,

without grief, like a history
healed of pain, "I outlive
all my children"

and walked to her communion
like an infant
stepping to love.

Note to Self

Fathers, too, deserve the seven times seventy rule. (Note to self: not a poem.) Nothing I ever said of you was true. Nothing said visited your pursed suffering I could only imagine. Father, you lived the sentence of my wanting you to be a hero, in those days when gods fell. I wanted you to be a god to my rescue. No, fathers should never be written unless we allow them, first, to be flesh, needing forgiveness. Only now, when your life glows at its end, I begin to see you.

First Snow and Living-room Blinds

This is how the heart burns, even here,
when light departs much too quickly
from the Don Valley, leaving the mind
almost wounded by surprise: a Christmas cactus,
multi-armed, flaming feisty fuchsia
on a keg of sweetened coconut, shredded,
Snowdrift Brand, saved for the aesthetics,
to complete a decorative adventure. At centre,
a fireplace, at left an ornamental book stack,
a standing lamp in amber, and CD basket
topped with Hot Summer Hits. For me,
the old economics of latitude framed in
a suburban window. And outside, at zero,
a bare oak, and ash trees wearing last leaves
in brilliant cold like insolent commas,
or else Holiday trees from home, long ago,
the branches cut then left to dry and shed,
awaiting the miracle of cotton snow –
postcard winters and carols we believed
enough to make the wishing-season more real.
This is how I hope it shall always be
when a wide and cloudless sky, anywhere,
fades to evening's quiet glow like prayer
grown past noise, and the gathering in
is ease, habit ripened to grace – Tiger
leisurely grooming her coat on a sofa,
preparing for sleep, her name borne
generously as rays silhouette
the sylvan script that ends all fullness.
And, suddenly, Justin's kindergarten
penmanship warms this far room – his rejoicing
over words he speaks then scribbles
with an unpractised hand – random lines
that sometimes cross and curve

to his meaning. Oh, but how his smile
rewrites a place, like blinds thrown open
to the gift of heaven raining first snow
makes every season just, so all right.

When a World Breaks

Greater tragedies have been averted because of what hits the kitchen-floor: diligently washed glasses and plates; bottles and jars that never survived the crossing from cupboard to counter or vice versa; the portentous egg that slipped past the well-practised grasp. First: the jolt from the sudden loss of what should be whole. Second: the expletive cum supplication depending on persuasion. Third: the survey of chaos – wondering which strand of one's living had finally snapped. Fourth: the half repentant clean up – shards swept out from every corner then committed to an impartial bin. Fifth: the ritual mop-up in elegiac metre when the floor is a stroked face. Sixth: the solemn house-warning, as from across a great divide, to be wary, still, of splinters. Seventh: the complete peace after a world breaks.

i feel myself releasing you

i feel myself releasing you and your going is slow, the way grief lingers with the hours, loitering at the door of every beginning, but never stepping past the old, only to save itself from losing exactly what must go… i feel myself releasing you, but your going is an agony i prefer to keep among the things i know, the way we guard our habits, even those we should let go, savouring their feel, loving so much and so like investors playing for returns. i feel myself releasing you and your going, this time, is an ancient song about losing what must be lost, put to death in grief itself – if loving is what we free, in each, to build a house with rooms enough for every love.

Visiting the Dragon

His is not a house you can let yourself in.
A steep gate fashioned
from Matura forests mans
a generous entrance that recalls, at first,
a middle-ages fortress – and why not,
having crossed Knight's Bridge
on an island home, too, of scripts
where mythic beasts and gods possess
streets and fictions no less real?
But when it thunders open,
sunrise vested in white cloud over
careering surf, and always
the scent of salt
greets you, disarming
even the dark,
then you know the universe
has turned a page
and the gate's span
is the measure of a great heart.

His is not a house you
can let yourself in,
only so welcome can be the gift
it gives, the coming to the other
that ends all awaited returns
and makes meeting
always absent of strangers,
a warmth that confounds
even the dogs,
their yelps straddling delight
and the required badness
of their station;
and as you are guided across
an uncluttered yard

roofed with bamboo,
you feel wheeled
into an astral dance
as his familiar round
of locutions orbits a schoolmaster's
praise, a bridge-maker's play
and parodied officialdom.
Then you realise, his is no house
to be let in.
Its fences girth earth and sky,
so once your feet connect
with that ample veranda perched
on the side of a ridge and bearing
its space like a possibility,
you feel upheld in the rest
of a gracious tree – no waste,
nothing artsy, just a floor
of simple timber, a ceiling
with the reach of matured teak,
leaves that peep in like neighbours,
and chairs unbashful of their wear,
but full of presences
and chorusing deep-run of roots that tap
a hidden river, far-travelled as Dakar,
but at home now
on the rim of Aldrick's city,
in green hills named after the over-
pouring plenty of water.
So, sitting across from Earl,
you know his is not a house…
when he clears his throat
and you hear the stoking of a forge
and, in those pre-speech sounds –
like a language reordering its rooms
or a taste of strong drink – a life
well-proofed to astonish;

and you know, too,
why even gods must fall
when those legs cross
and you find yourself
on the other side of the camera
and you know
this is not just a movie
when he asks,
"So what have you been doing?"
Then, laughter erupts,
breaking the screen
and re-youthing time to bless
flesh and blood to climb
where dragons fly.

A Place

I

None of this is exotic. You arrive
at a place. The landscape is not strange:
a valley, miles of brazen green;
a river plays hide and seek through trees
and bridges snap territorially at wheels;
a pot-hound emerges from a track,
its tail whipping joy; then the surprise
of a solitary shack, a woman and child
drifting in a hammock, the estate behind
wearing decline like a sentence,
you first think, then retract –
their peace too real to foreclose a future.
Then after descending flights
of forest, a village appears:
a flock of ducks vests a yard
and makes a home a shrine. Wonder
lingers as you cruise past a field
tonsured at goalposts naked of nets
stationed like gates into a world
where a neighbourhood of shops sport
product signs like medals and men,
installed under cool eaves, record
your passing with practised nonchalance;
where children race blinkered
along a street that plunges
into a gleaming sea.

II

The place from where the road descends
to Grande Riviere villagers call *Topside*,
as if they dwell below the world, or else
bear the whole of it upon their backs –
carrying all who suppose themselves large.
Cross the bridge where a shallow river, wide
enough to earn its name, strolls seaward,
sheltered by bamboo. Hear some small,
sad thing cry in your heart, asking
you to reach into its cradle, joyfully
lift it to your face and, in the grace
of that seeing, bless it, and be blessed
for travelling on to a life casually
ordering itself, finding its way, knowing,
like you know, the sound of the ocean,
and that you, too, are its gift and mirror,
and what now croons at your breast
is the child of all ends – and beginning is
this holding, the other side of its rest.

III

This is your climate – its charm
familiar like the man you see
walking his birds, a cage balanced
in each hand, his pausing to watch you
drive by then park beside a shop
where regulars congregate
for their morning shot,
and a young woman breezes in, comfortable
in her nightie, to buy cheese
by the ounce, and bread, then gathers
her purchases without paying,
beneath a sign that reads: *No Credit*.
Her buoyant *Later*, as she turns to leave,
the trust accepted by the adolescent,
meticulously dressed for school,
his face already inscrutable as he directs
a proprietorial, *Yes, Miss*, to you;
your money offered before you ask:
Express, please, to which he answers,
a little flatly: *Try next door.*
We doh sell papers here.
And all of a sudden you feel a stranger,
and you wonder what trembles
like a bird in your palm.

IV

Next door, a woman seated
behind the counter
interrupts her conversation
on a cell-phone she mutes
against her breast to let you know:
Papers late today.
She had anticipated your question;
but you linger, a little uncertain
as to what *late* might mean –
an hour, two hours, midday? –
though you know this habit
of imprecision, the saving of what time
itself cannot master.
She is so electric with her talk
and, in that light, you decide
on another purchase – a sunny cake
in the sparse cosmos
of the glass case.
She rises in exaggerated slow
motion to serve.
Her smile is for the person
on the other end of the phone
now hugged to her ear
by a shoulder.
And, as she dreamily bags the cake
and forages under the counter
for change, adds, like a bonus: *Dearie,*
Skippy van break down in Grande.
No papers today.

V

Back on a concrete pavement
that ends abruptly
as though some idea
ran out on itself,
you hear laughter behind your back,
as talk goes on,
and you smile at your late
realization that *Skippy*
is the one on the other end,
and his not showing
the real news of her day – his voice
bringing the one thing necessary,
Joy! And that is the light
you stand in when the youth
now stationed across the road
sees you and nods a recognition
before boarding a van,
its idle almost seismic, the driver
leaning forward, wanting to go,
and as they rattle off,
the cheerful shout from the tray,
Later Auntie!
And with the phone hugged
to her ear, the woman appears,
waves her answer,
and you witness another love –
simply, an agreement for one
shop to be without – to make all
their homecomings sure.

VI

Everybody here is family.
Pride punctuates her declaration,
her way of confirming
the surprise your face registers.
That there is Denzel – speaking
as though he never left.
My brother first-born.
Brains too bad.
Then gesturing to the sea –
He goin to go far –
her conviction, a faith beyond
defence or threat,
empty even of loss – this going
that is never really leaving,
a belonging not tied to shores,
claimed for this nephew
with *brains* from what is
already also hers, a home.
Now her *Walk good* blesses
your stay in this far region
of your island before returning
to her call with *Skippy.*
Her assurance to him, *I right here*,
leaving you this riddle of arrival:
De distance is here,
and making the word
of casual affection – *familee* –
directed to you by a limer
perched recklessly at the entrance
of the shop on an up-ended crate
seem an honest welcome.

VII

I have been considering this:
the being without that is having;
yes, the bounty that is not owning, yes,
and, too, the losing that is the gaining all;
these twin-islands, these Americas,
this globe – rock and sand and
earth and river and sea, stars and wind
and cold, yes even that. Claim it – we,
the multitude of a word, in a word,
by whatever name, a universe – in one word.
You can say it – familee – with and without
the histories and treaties,
with and without the buying
and selling, the gains and losses,
the discoveries and rebellions,
thefts and murders and births,
without intonation and coded irises,
flags, artillery, and dances, without
dates of betrayal and arrival,
alphabets, libraries and irrigation,
without decrees and anthems, GNP and geographies –
yes, without heroes and IQ scores,
botany and philosophy and homeland security,
chromosomes, HIV screens and degrees,
without passport and twitter account,
BBM and religion,
Index of Economic Freedom,
without UN mediation
and immigration.
Can we speak that belonging word
as freely as that man who said to me,
You look like a Darbeau.
That is your people? And when I said no,
he shrugged it off and said:

That is nothing, Miss.
Yuh take after them.

VIII

And what about there? – 145 years
into *God Save the Queen* and
a red maple leaf, there
where even squirrels perfect the art
of scurrying along wire highways
that crisscross yards, those colonies
of trees much more a home.
And what about it? These once pristine
wooden fences daily darkening
like living bark, and the gateways
raccoons open between chain-
linked divides to walk single file along
borders of yards – proprietorial
tracks that make owners gasp.
What about them? There, too,
the wind in leaves sounds like surf
and summer is 32 degrees –
the equivalent of a home
now fifty, and with a flag. What of it?
The red, the white of it.
And the black. There, the earth
is dark and nurtures things.
Fifty, they say, is the age of gold –
not the fantasia of El Dorado.
It begins the learning to walk
between worlds – unfettered
like air. Even, here.

IX

There is a singing here that is sometimes rain –
not always. A god without name makes a way
across the mountain where Rose Hill's houses
squat before a turquoise sea that every day
marries the horizon becoming, simply, heaven.
It must be a god passing, the One that slipped
through the crowd and vanished into thin air,
leaving hearts burning with the question:
Who are you? And the raw desire to be near.
It must be the deity of that insatiable poverty.
What but a love so longed for could silence
quarrelsome zinc sheets, soothe midday heat,
remind the ear of her listening for mysteries
the wind shares with trees, so sweet
they weep.

X

The guesthouse sits like an amethyst on the hill.
At first you think what is precious is its veranda
that overlooks the bay where leatherbacks nest.
The cheap privilege that comes with a panorama
intoxicates and vision is mere romance that flirts
with the fiction of a return to something simpler.
So you stumble before the truth you came to see –
plain as an ancient reptile emerging from the sea.

Amethyst, legend tells, prevents drunkenness.
Lilac is the hue your grandmother, Sybil,
painted her rooms before she passed, as if she
wanted her senses crystal clear at St. Peter's gate.
Turtles and amethysts sign her faith: reality
is the vision of a hoped for happiness.

XI

Few may accept this: Time is Grande Riviere.
In fact, it chose to write its meanings on endless
pages of sea and blank beaches, on the lines
in fishermen's hands; in the crevices of rock
it hid mysteries, on the new parchment of babies
and tender leaves, on the long scroll of a single road;
its records kept on rusty ridges of galvanize sheets
and laths of rickety bridges, on the smooth face
of river stones and in furrows of the old. It wrote
among the garden rows, left signs in spider webs
and tea cups, in dreams it spoke prophecies,
gave the Gospel to fresh streams, and etched
eternity on leatherbacks. Each year, they labour
from the deep to lay the future there.

XII

Just so you know, it is time
for words to flow
from your hands like blood.
This is the hour
when an early silence sings
every song, chants, mantras
and hymns – for all manner
of things.
You hear the ocean's churn,
ciçada's wail, tanagers
working at their nest
behind the refrigerator,
and the mongrel *Wheyhim* scratching
contentedly on the steps;
you hear with each leaf's fall
the sermon of a world
without end,
and this moment is all –
your surrender to what quickens
in the roots of every tree,
even the termite-riddled avocado
you saw, and marvelled at
its stubborn offer of fruit,
dying the only way it knew how
to live – full-fold, wholly
in praise of its being.

XIII

No real living is ease.
Even in calm, the surf shuffles
its beaches, as any welcome
is a labour to be worked
over again and again
with greater love,
and salvation the *rest*
of that employment,
infinite as the sea –
your first meditation.

Gather this: the tern's
wisdom is its communal
resting and, in flight, the crucifixion
of its journeys across land
and ocean – always travelling
mercies, the currency
of all resurrections to the new
ground we reach
by the sweat and blood
and tears of every ancestor
un-failed for trying,
even in gross error, to root
wherever there is earth
and light and water – everything
here – but fearing still
the sentence of a threatening
nothing, dis-
ease of the faithless
when faith seems too small
a seed to hope in bloom-
ing rockstone, Roach's brutal
creed when time itself
was so green.

Benediction is remedy or
true sanctity – the love
that loves for nothing
and so forgives and gives
like this heart-maker's art
that weds you,
prefers your rooms, finds
in the cadence of your voice song
enough for every season,
and this is the same
on any shore where the sun
also rises and falls,
and you come to know
with easier wonder
there is never any controlling
the silver, only the grace
of letting go… it is so,
it is… will be…
so ordinary as looking
through your bedroom window
and seeing white egrets
assembled on the lawn,
and not feeling overtaken,
or else the wound of realising you lost
your chance at heaven,
as when you saw those running
shadows through the streets
of Trujillo's Santiago
and thought they were ghosts
until dawn revealed them
to be Haiti's children chasing
after work while their hosts
slept a crude ease.

But those seraphic birds
that morning, spread wide to feed

like detached beneficiaries
in the wake of Sunil's mower –
his Calvary whenever it rains
on this patch of Caroni,
where soil imprinted with cane-
cutters passing is not so agreeable –
but as he advances, pushing
with force for a hill, drawing
on the copy of grass, fresh lines,
and you know then astonishment,
the balm that cures verse to scripture
as when newness opens unexpectedly
like unfurled wings, spotless
as a baptismal dress
redeems space. And, with gratitude,
you read there what every heart
like a restless sea beats to discover:
the One metre we all share
that anchors every peace.

Siparia Mela

On the day God died,
molecules, too, sighed
It is finished. It is finished –

the discoverer's
malady of single signs,
adrift in a jaundiced channel,

dressed with Sargasso
poultices – *his* water
with berries uncured
of a history.

No more now,
as when a sky flips the night's page
or a woman spreads

freshly laundered sheets
on the line of a shore
sweetened by faiths.

On such a day,
the very air exhales
and emptied

of itself makes space
that wary time may be born
again. Yes,

it is finished. Today,
the sea broke her water –
and a sundry chorus

makes bhakti
to Soparee Mai. Rosaries,
jap mala, misbaha…

beads for berries,
crimson as the blood
of a God, a man

of a woman born. Dies.
Today, you will be
in Paradise. Death is no more.

This is it – a mela
for La Divina, the way feet
process to every drum to-

day. Long landed. We
cross. Speak in tongues
on these ragged shores, well-

familiar with what death bags,
my lines, unforgetful, even now,
of those who, too soon,

drank the ocean's salt,
made their tombstones
these short-crested waves.

Mother, small mirror
of who we are, but see
too dimly,

as the lean faith of prayers
holds its carnival
on all our graves, un-swaddle

your new-born race
to greet uplift seasons, free
as birds fly untethered

by any sound or fury
into the wondrous web
of morning.

I want nothing of the sea

Today, I think no more of oceans,
cobalt shroud of ancestors, all
quarter of my claim to any name.
I do not think of waves today,

though my skin reeks salt,
flavour of islands, an El Dorado
mistaken for gold – my eyes gritty
with the hope of a pearl.

No, I want nothing of the sea,
divider of the left behind, road
without signs, inconsumable water
for thirst, ribbed highway

with no roof to house the want
of a home. I will have
nothing of oceans, today. No ports
to imagined countries,

for what is hardest is arrivals, and
returns are always why we leave.
I want only this Rock against storms
though the guns rain every day,

our pillars – sand – and those charged
to open doors speak only wind
to sate a hunger that gathers
to a hurricane's roar.

I want nothing of beaches,
shrines that tempt distance
for the love of a page. Today,
when my blood knows

no sanctuary can hold me,
and horizons spring from this earth
where roots thrust down, and deep
hears the call of deep.

I want nothing of the sea, today.

Dear Poetry

Don't get me wrong,
but today
I have a bone to pick
with you.
I not ungrateful
how you choose me
outta everybody,
how you decide to come
and live with me,
give me your company.
I not ungrateful how
yuh take me, bring me
to a life so sweet
not even ripe mango
could beat.

So I not complaining
that is under my roof
you choose to stay,
three times by plenty
call my name.
Truth be told,
I was never so happy
to know how
is so long you holding
candle for me,
that yuh never change
your mind about me.

And is with my two eye
wide open I say yes –
this is my life, no more
running away,
no more making circles,

dizzying mihself,
chasing after mih own tail
only to end-up right,
back with you
again.

And now I so full
I caring more poem-
pickney than I know how,
and these days
I so forget mihself
mirror can't see me –
so-and-so want to know
if I take up and 'migrate
and dem malicious mouth
spreading rumour
that is dead
I come and dead.

What they don't know
is my days busy –
picking up after you,
serving at your table,
gathering every crumb
that hit ground, sweeping
out every corner
so nothing lose –
not one bit of you –
making this life
into to a singing
that could shine stars,
warm the sun, cool
breeze, even heal
that two-timing lisp
on Anansi – true-
true, all-day-

all-night spinning
your light.

I not complaining,
though I must let you know
it not always easy
to grow the words
we make together,
and sometimes lines
raise eyes, shake worlds –
cause me and all to turn.
And though people think
I stupidy to stay with you,
I know better:
is carry I have to carry
with you the weight of us
being here together.

So this time,
I not saying I not staying;
but tonight, I feel
I want to kick off my shoes,
put up my feet and sip
soothing lime laced
with a heavy-han' pour
of good island rum –
and a dash of Angostura
for the bitter. I want
to close my eyes
and feel the Atlantic
wash over me.
And I want to listen
to Etta belting out
one and a thousand times
that unsheltered line – *At last*
my love has come along.

Tonight Love, I want you
to write me
a poem.

Desire

She wanted her rooms to be light
so she polished her atoms.

She wanted peace so she dug deep
and listened to her noise.

She wanted joy unending so she learnt
the applause of leaves.

She wanted hope so she traded shoes
for earth-clad roots.

She wanted faith so she counted
every second a miracle.

She wanted change so she became
an august hurricane.

She dreamed a new world
so she wore its variant blossoms.

She wanted love so she married
a world and settled in to serve.

She wanted to be a poet so she drew a circle
and welcomed in the cosmos.

POSTSCRIPT

Waves

Every beach rewrites itself, wipes away yesterday, not to forget, but that memory may be free to invent. For a beach, waves are a sure salvation, unsettling, as any god would shun the tyranny in permanence. Each morning the tide turns a new page like a child blows a spit-washed slate, singing: *Jumbie, jumbie, fly away*. They always return – the words – to travel this line between land and sea, until, mercifully, breakers steal their thunder, salt and reshuffle their chapters to tell greater fictions.

Epiphany

There will come a time when stillness
is all the motion you will ever need
to take you where the real going leads.

In that one place – it may be a room
small as a cave, turgid with the hours
of every age, hosting the simplicity

that makes all leavings seem so routine –
the seeking, asking, knocking to find
what keeps company with the ordinary –

in that place, fragrant with your living,
you will begin at last to see
the meaning of it all. Right here: peace.

ABOUT THE AUTHOR

Jennifer Rahim is Trinidadian. She is a Senior Lecturer in Literature in the Department of Literary, Cultural and Communication Studies at the University of the West Indies, St. Augustine. Her essays on Caribbean literature have appeared in *MaComère*, *The Journal of West Indian Literature, Small Axe*, *Anthurium*, *TOUT MOUN* and *BIM*. She edited, with Barbara Lalla, *Beyond Borders: Cross Culturalism and the Caribbean Canon* (UWI Press 2009) and *Created in the West Indies: Caribbean Perspectives on V.S. Naipaul* (Ian Randle, 2010). Her poetry collections include: *Between the Fence and the Forest* (Peepal Tree Press, *2002)*, *Approaching Sabbaths* (Peepal Tree Press, 2009) and *Redemption Rain* (TSAR, 2011). She has one collection of short stories, *Songster and Other Stories* (Peepal Tree Press, 2007). *Approaching Sabbaths* was awarded a Casa de las Américas Prize in 2010.

ALSO BY JENNIFER RAHIM

Between the Fence and the Forest
ISBN: 9781900715270; pp. 88; pub. 2002; £7.99

Comparing herself to a douen, a mythical being from the Trinidadian forests whose head and feet face in different directions, Jennifer Rahim's poems explore states of uncertainty both as sources of discomfort and of creative possibility.

The poems explore a Trinidad finely balanced between the forces of rapid urbanisation and the constantly encroaching green chaos of tropical bush, whose turbulence regularly threatens a fragile social order, and whose people, as the descendants of slaves and indentured labourers, are acutely resistant to any threat to clip their wings and fence them in.

In more personal poems, Rahim explores the contrary urges to a neat security and to an unfettered sense of freedom and her attraction to the forest "where tallness is not the neighbour's fences/ and bigness is not the swollen houses/ that swallow us all". It is, though, a place where the bushplanter "seeing me grow branches/ draws out his cutting steel and slashes my feet/ since girls can never become trees".

Approaching Sabbaths
ISBN: 9781845231156; pp. 132; pub. 2009; £8.99

Winner of a Casa de las Américas Prize 2010 – one of Latin America's oldest and most prestigious literary awards – *Approaching Sabbaths* was described by the jury as a collection that "captures a sense of the complexities of historical, social and cultural aspects of the contemporary Caribbean".

The poems move seamlessly between the inwardly confessional, which show an acute sensitivity to the distinctive subjectivities of an immediate circle of family, friends and neighbours, and a powerful sense of Trinidadian place and history. Few have written more movingly or perceptively of what can vex the relationship between daughters and mothers, or with such a mixture of compassion and baffled rage about a daughter's relationship to her father. If Sylvia Plath comes to mind, acknowledged in the poem 'Lady Lazarus in the Sun', the comparison does Rahim no disfavours; Rahim's voice and world is entirely her own. There is in her work a near perfect balance between the disciplined craft of the poems, and their capacity to deal with the most traumatic of experiences in a cool, reflective way. Equally, she has the capacity to make of the ordinary something special and memorable.

Whilst the threat and reality of fragmentation – of psyches, of lives, of a nation – is ever present, the compassion and the shape and order of the poems provide a saving frame of wholeness. Poem after poem offers memorable phrases, such as the description of the killers of a boy as "mere children,/ but twisted like neglected fields of cane".

Songster and Other Stories
ISBN: 9781845230487; pp. 120; pub. 2007; £8.99

Rahim's stories move between the present and the past to make sense of the tensions between image and reality in contemporary Trinidad. The contemporary stories show the traditional, communal world in retreat before the forces of local and global capitalism. A popular local fisherman is gunned down when he challenges the closure of the beach for a private club catering to white visitors and the new elite; the internet becomes a rare safe place for an AIDS sufferer to articulate her pain; cocaine has become the scourge even of the rural communities. But the stories set thirty years earlier in the childhood of the narrating "I" reveal that the "old-time" Trinidad was already breaking up. The old pieties about nature symbolised by the folk-figure of "Papa Bois" are powerless to prevent the ruthless plunder of the forests; communal stability has already been uprooted by the pulls towards emigration, and any sense that Trinidad was ever edenic is undermined by images of the destructive power of alcohol and the casual presence of paedophilic sexual abuse.

Rahim's Trinidad, is though, as her final story makes clear, the creation of a writer who has chosen to stay, who is highly conscious that her perspective is very different from those who have taken home away in a suitcase, or who visit once a year. Her Trinidad is "not a world in my head like a fantasy", but the island that "lives and moves in the bloodstream". Her reflection on the nature of small island life is as fierce and perceptive as Jamaica Kincaid's in *A Small Place*, but it comes from and arrives at a quite opposite place. What Rahim finds in her island is a certain existential insouciance and the capacity of its people, whatever their material circumstance, to commit to life in the knowledge of its bitter-sweetness.